We Must Join China's New Silk Road

Victory Requires Understanding Your British Enemy

by Robert Ingraham

Sept. 11—On Saturday, Sept. 9, 2017, *Executive Intelligence Review* sponsored a day-long event in Manhattan, titled "The Russian 'Hack' Inside Job: Who's Trying To Destroy the Presidency and Start a World War with Russia?" That event, moderated by Dennis Speed, featured presentations by three guests: longtime *EIR* Editorial Board member William F. Wertz, Jr., accompanied by William Binney and Ray McGovern, both leading members of the Veteran Intelligence Professionals for Sanity (VIPS).

William Binney is a retired thirty-year veteran of the National Security Agency and the subject of the recent documentary film *A Good American*. Ray McGovern was a top analyst with the Central Intelligence Agency for twenty-seven years.

Although efforts to sabotage and destroy the Trump Presidency will continue, the repercussions of what was presented at the Sept. 9 New York event now make any intention to continue with the "Russia-gate" attacks on the Trump Administration extremely untenable, as well as risky for all those involved in the attack. In the course of their two presentations and the ensuing discussion, Messrs. McGovern and Binney presented a devastating critique of the allegations that the Russians interfered in the U.S. election and "hacked" DNC computers. In one sense, this was the "final word" on all of the lies that have been circulated by the establishment media in recent months. This event accomplished a powerful intervention, one which now opens the possibility for defeating the enemies of President Trump and securing a new U.S. strategic orientation.

The Current Battlefield

What took place in New York must be viewed within the context of the global battle, now underway, as to the future for both America and all of the world. Out of great crises, great opportunities arise, and leadership is tested.

Let us review the current situation:

Already, it was the suffering of the American people, and the hopes raised by the Trump campaign, that led to the election of Donald Trump ten months ago. Now, the anguish of the millions of Americans who are living through the effects of hurricanes Harvey and Irma is crying out to our nation's leaders, calling for "action, and action now."

EDITORIAL

At the same time, global events have reached a point where they must now go one way or another. War or Peace? President Trump's cooperation with Russia in Syria has brought that war to a point where victory and peace are within sight. Trump's stated intention to improve relations with Russia and China has moved forward. Yet, even in the face of this progress, efforts continue, and are escalating, to provoke war in the Korean peninsula, to poison U.S.-Russian relations, and to push the world into a geometry of heightened crisis-management.

Overhanging all of this is the Damocles Sword of the London-Wall Street speculative financial system, now bankrupt according to any traditional legitimate accounting method, and overripe for a collapse worse than 2008.

We are at an unprecedented moment. This is a crisis. But it is also an opportunity. All of the "Russia-gate" attacks, all of the Charlottesville-related "racism" allegations, all of the anti-Trump hatred can be swept away if leadership is provided now. Justice and opportunity for Americans can be secured if leadership is provided now. The loss and suffering of millions can be alleviated if leadership is provided now.

William Binney (left) and Ray McGovern.

All that is required to accomplish this, is for growing numbers of Americans to finally "listen to the wise words of Lyndon LaRouche"—to recognize that the type of leadership that is now required is exactly that which Lyndon LaRouche has provided for the last forty-odd years. The need for global monetary reform was first addressed by LaRouche forty years ago in his International Development Bank proposal; the great projects now under consideration, such as the Trans-aqua project, the Thailand (Kra) Canal, and others, were proposed by LaRouche twenty, thirty, or more years ago. A comprehensive, national water-management system, which would protect against both floods and drought, was put forward by LaRouche in the 1980s; the murderous drug epidemic that is ruining and killing our youth was taken on by LaRouche in the 1970s with the publication of *Dope, Inc.*, and he spearheaded a fight against drugs in the 1980s.

The list goes on; but the key truth that must be grasped is that all of the life-and-death crises we are now facing are *solvable*. Leadership, as discussed by H. Graham Lowry in his article on Abraham Lincoln in this current issue of *EIR* page 8, is the key ingredient. LaRouche has provided that leadership, and it is time for people to listen to him. The New York *EIR* event is the latest intervention by LaRouche, operating through his Manhattan Project, to create new potentials for victory. Those now conspiring to destroy the Trump Presidency suffered a huge defeat on September 9, and this now creates new possibilities for moving forward with an agenda of peace and economic development.

Critical Controversy and Deadly Weakness

It is impossible to win a war if you don't know whom you are fighting. One of the greatest weaknesses to be found among the defenders of President Trump is in their continually referring to the "Deep State" as the source for the attacks on the President. On Sept. 9, Will Wertz provoked a great deal of controversy—and anxiety—with a presentation that correctly named the historic, as well as current, strategic enemy of the United States as the British empire. Drawing on historical and economic material discovered and developed by the LaRouche movement over many years, Wertz demonstrated not merely a two-hundred-year ongoing conflict between Britain and America, but the axiomatic and conflicting outlooks of the American republican-impulse tradition versus the British imperial view. The details of what Wertz articulated (as well as the full speeches of Binney and McGovern) may be viewed in the full video of the event. Here, it is sufficient to state that Wertz presented a concise historical overview, beginning with George Washington, and going on through Abraham Lincoln, William McKinley, Franklin Roosevelt, and John Kennedy, of the evidence that the British empire has always been the mortal enemy of the principles of the Declaration of Independence and the United States Constitution.

A number of participants at the New York event were perturbed or even outraged at what Wertz presented. Generally, the objections took two forms: either that Britain is our ally, and it is unacceptable to attack it in this way; or, that Britain today is no longer a major power, and to accuse it of having significant influence over U.S. policy-making or the U.S. intelligence community, is absurd.

One could answer these objections by presenting a laundry list of "evidence" of Britain's anti-American designs—such as Tony Blair's role in the first Iraq War or the role of Christopher Steele, MI6, and GCHQ in the current efforts to destroy President Trump—but there is a larger issue to address.

There is a great weakness among many American patriots. At the worst, it takes the form of Anglophilia; but a lesser, if still fatal, weakness is an illiteracy as regards American history and the true nature of world affairs over the last two-and-a-half centuries. Most Americans simply don't know what it was all about. They don't grasp the *Mission of America*, as it was conceived by Washington, Hamilton and Lincoln. They also have no comprehension of the *oligarchical principle* and what motivates the controllers of empire. As a result, they don't see the battlefield today for what it truly is. They are crippled in how they fight. It is precisely the themes developed by Wertz in his presentation which are vital and which must be fought out with every American.

9/11

There will be many repercussions from Saturday's New York event. One of these, undoubtedly, will be to refocus attention, once again, on 9/11.

In response to a question about 9/11, William Binney stated, "They had all the data to stop 9/11 before 9/11 in their databases, and didn't know it. It was all there. Even the date of the attack was given. Even the date of the attack was given!" And he went on to say, "In fact, I think, according to some sources, they had actually had somebody in there who was saying the attack was coming but didn't know the date or anything, and they were trying to report that but they couldn't—NSA wouldn't let them report it."

The LaRouche organization, together with many other men and women of courage, has battled for sixteen years to expose the government lies about 9/11, and to hold Saudi Arabia and Great Britain to account as the perpetrators of that crime. The evidence of Saudi/British involvement is conclusive. By addressing this directly and publicly at the New York event, from his vantage point as an expert and the author of many of the data-mining and intelligence-gathering programs utilized by the NSA, Binney has reopened a critical flank, one which holds out hope for justice. One thing is certain: The enemies of our nation are not sleeping soundly tonight.

Crises—and the tragedy that often accompanies them—are also singularities, times when people unite around that which is important. It is often at just such moments when great things might be accomplished. As the flood-waters recede from hurricanes Harvey and Irma, a new hope is being born. An aroused people are acting to save the nation. We witnessed an inkling of the power of that future on Sept. 9 in New York.

LAROUCHE

Don't Discuss It—Just *Do* It!

Sept. 7—All of a sudden it has become blindingly obvious that Russia's President Vladimir Putin—in the spirit of his spiritual ancestor, France's "Spider King" Louis XI—has been weaving and reweaving a web of potentially close economic cooperation between North and South Korea and Russia—and with China and other partners as well.

This was the original "LaRouche Plan" for peace in the Korean Peninsula, which worked until the day that it was sabotaged in 2002 through "outside forces" working with then-Vice President Cheney, and afterwards President Obama. Putin has been weaving this web with indispensable support from China—but also, it appears, from certain forces in Washington.

When this was brought to the attention of Lyndon LaRouche, he said, "Don't discuss it. Don't rehash the details. Don't waste any time—just do it! And by doing it—*Now!*—you will force the hand of those forces in Washington who oppose it. They will be exposed, ready to be neutralized."

At just the same moment, the worst Atlantic hurricane ever recorded, with 180 mph winds peaking at almost 300 mph, has been moving through the Caribbean, leaving some of the British colonial islands in ruins unimaginable for the 21st Century. The Prime Minister of Barbuda, for example, said that 90% of its buildings had been destroyed and 60% of its population was homeless. The British masters had done absolutely nothing to prepare for the deluge—but why would they?

But the U.S. government, led by President Trump, is aware, is on top of the situation, and is mobilizing the appropriate resources for Florida and other threatened areas—and this in turn will permit the population, both the first-responders and citizen-volunteers, to show the heroism they showed so magnificently in Houston. We will respond as required. We will rebuild as rapidly as can be done. Everything has changed since Katrina and Sandy.

In the Caribbean, the United States must offer the full-bore Army Corps of Engineers program which Lyndon LaRouche and former President Bill Clinton proposed for Haiti after the 2010 earthquake. Monster-President Obama shot that plan down, so that Haiti, still in ruins today, is now working with China towards rebuilding the country.

But our urgent and necessary rebuilding must be only the springboard for a full national infrastructure program, beginning now with masses of Federal credit and in cooperation with China. Not only will we limit the scope of such storm-related disasters in the future, but we will transform our entire economy from the disaster we inherited from Bush and Obama, into the great agro-industrial power which the world and all Americans need now.

On this, Lyndon LaRouche said again, "Don't waste time discussing it. Just do it! And we will see who tries to prevent it—it will be obvious!"

EIR**Contents**

www.larouchepub.com Volume 44, Number 37, September 15, 2017

*Cover
This Week*

Workers at a railway construction site in China.

photo/Xinhua

WE MUST JOIN CHINA'S NEW SILK ROAD

2 REPORT FROM NEW YORK
Victory Requires Understanding Your Enemy
by Robert Ingraham

5 LAROUCHE
Don't Discuss It—Just *Do* It!

I. The Return of the Human Factor

7 A Sublime Moment in Houston
by Dan Leach

8 RE-CREATING THE REPUBLIC
How Abraham Lincoln Organized Victory for the Union
by H. Graham Lowry

19 In the Garden of Gethsemane
by Lyndon H. LaRouche, Jr.
January 1990

22 Failure of Leadership Caused Hurricane Harvey Disaster
by Evelyn Lantz

II. We Must Join China's New Silk Road

24 CHINA AND RUSSIA DRIVE NEW PARADIGM
BRICS Summit and Eastern Economic Forum Give Hope to Mankind
by Michael Billington

31 Africa: Transaqua Project Gains Momentum
by Claudio Celani

36 EDITORIAL
Largest Mexican Earthquake In a Century
Time to Forecast Natural Disasters and Defend Mankind!
by Benjamin L. Deniston

A Sublime Moment in Houston

by Dan Leach

Aug. 6—Those of us in the LaRouche movement in Houston were witness not only to a terrible tragedy over the last week, but also to the manifestation of a powerful and profound principle. Not only did literally thousands of first responders—police, firemen, National Guard, Coast Guard, and other agencies—from as far away as New York and Boston pour in to help in the rescue operations, risking their lives repeatedly—but many more thousands of ordinary people came here

U.S. Coast Guard

U.S. Marine officers performing search and rescue operations in Lumberton, Texas, Aug. 31, 2017, in which they rescued over 300 people in this operation alone.

from all over the country with boats, canoes, trucks, or anything that could float or get through high water, to help save the lives of people they had never met.

One policeman and several civilians did, indeed, lose their lives while doing this. It was deeply inspiring to see so many examples of selfless giving, cooperation, and downright heroism which the emergency brought out.

Everyone, from news reporters to ordinary residents, sensed that, in that moment, there were no political, racial, or religious differences—there were only human beings who were in danger or suffering and needed help. People who had just been evacuated, and had lost their own homes, were back out there immediately helping to get others to safety.

Perhaps the most poignant image was that of a "redneck"—maybe part of the famous so-called "Cajun Navy" who came over from Louisiana with their boats— with a big Confederate flag on the side of his boat, rescuing African-American and Hispanic families. Any notion one may have had less than a month ago, in the

aftermath of the events in Charlottesville, that America was hopelessly divided and engulfed in hate and paranoia, seemed to vanish.

But the tragic deaths of Donald and Rochelle Rogers, the father and stepmother of LaRouche PAC Policy Committee member Kesha Rogers, in the aftermath of the storm, involve a deeper principle. Yes, they were indeed tragic, because so unnecessary—if only we had lived up to the legacy of past generations and made the investments in the infrastructure projects which would have mitigated the effects of the flooding, they would never have died. And the fact that when they died, they were attempting to drive to a nearby town to help a relative whom they believed to be in danger, not only speaks to the beauty of their souls, but heightens the tragedy.

But there is a profound sense in everyone touched by this and the other stories of human loss, that we must commit ourselves to a future in which this never happens again. As in war, where there inevitably is suffering and death—if the peace is truly won, the sacrifice of those lives was not in vain.

There is the palpable presence of a spirit in all of this, both of tremendous sadness and the frailty of human existence—but at the same time of the goodness and potential nobility in most people.

It is the mission of true political leadership to evoke this and marshal it to achieve its great historical purpose. This is the mission for which our association, because we understand this, is so uniquely qualified and so needed.

How Abraham Lincoln Organized Victory for the Union

by H. Graham Lowry

The following article was originally published in EIR *vol. 30, no. 33, of August 29, 2003. The article was published posthumously, about one month after the death of its author, historian Graham Lowry, a long-time associate of Lyndon LaRouche, and author of* How the Nation Was Won: America's Untold Story, Volume I, 1630-1754. *The piece, as published at that time, was taken from notes left by Graham for an article he intended to write, as well as from classes he delivered in Arlington, Virginia, New York City, and Baltimore, Maryland. It was compiled by his late wife Pamela into the form published in 2003. It is reprinted now, in a slightly edited version, due to its extraordinary relevance to key matters confronting both the United States and the world today. Of particular note are its insights into the question of leadership, as Graham discusses in his examination of Abraham Lincoln.*

The United States in 1860 was on the brink of total destruction. Abraham Lincoln knew it; a handful of other patriots knew it on one level or another; and the plotters seeking to overthrow the government were becoming bolder every day. What was the threat to the constitutional republic in 1860? Secession? The spread of slavery? Civil war? These dangers by then had been broadly recognized— even openly promoted by leading Southerners. But these were secondary aspects of a planned *coup d'état]* to bring the constitutional republic of the United States to an end. Abraham Lincoln dared to shoulder the unique responsibility for simultaneously defending the republic from its enemies and creating the conditions for a lasting peace. As he said in his Cooper Union address in 1860:

> Neither let us be slandered from our duty by false accusations against us, nor frightened from it by menaces of destruction to the Government, nor of dungeons to ourselves. Let us have faith that right makes might, and in that faith let us, to the end, dare to do our duty as we understand it.

commissioned by the United States Historical Society

After the Union Army took control of Richmond, the confederate capital, Lincoln insisted on visiting Richmond in April, 1865, with his son Tad, to heal the wounds of war and reunite the nation. This statue was unveiled in April 2003.

Who was this Lincoln, this ugly duckling who told rollicking frontier tales and wrote in the beautiful language of the English Renaissance?

The Mind of Abraham Lincoln

Now, what I am going to try to do, is to enable you to actually exist within the mind of Abraham Lincoln for a while, and, of course, if you keep working on it, you can keep doing it for a long time. Not merely is Lincoln one of the most significant examples of the leadership principle in the American historical tradition; but he is that, anywhere in world history. In a crisis such as this nation and the world face today, the advantage that you have, is that you can turn to a model of the leadership principle, in the sense that I'm going to demonstrate with Lincoln. And you will find that all kinds of, say, lieutenants, and rank and file, good citizens, and so forth, whose efforts on behalf of keeping something called "human," something worthwhile about human life going forward, do it through their grandchildren, either literally or figuratively. We have the responsibility now to ensure the future of those children two generations into the future. You don't wait around and see if they can work it out when they're twenty years old, because by that time there may not be a future.

And that is what makes you human: that you take the responsibility to extend the efforts that people made before you, and you start projecting them forward, and working to ensure them for another good span of time to come. And then, you find that these historical people are with you, not in some mumbo-jumbo sense, but in the sense that they will be resources that you can bring back into the war, that will live again through you, and that you'll be stronger because of them. And then people will recognize: "Wait a minute, there's something different about this person. This person represents something I can trust, and something that I will follow."

And that is what people did see in Lincoln. It took a while for him to develop it, but when he did, it was unmistakable. It's why we defeated the British-inspired slave empire called the Confederacy, and kept it from destroying the only republic in the history of the world, a Constitutional Republic, that had as its principle, the sacred creative potential of each individual citizen. I'm sure you've read something about the principle of the general welfare, the good of the whole society, and that the only purpose of government is to ensure that for the present and the future as well. If you have a government that starts saying, "Who can we go kill tomorrow? Let's find someplace where we don't like the way the people look, or the color of their skin, and then we'll bomb 'em! Torch 'em! Imprison 'em! Create dictatorships, create an empire." That's not the United States of America. That is not our mission in history.

And the people who've known what the mission was, have been the people who have come to the fore when it was threatened. Lincoln had to do it. Franklin Delano Roosevelt had to do it, and Lyndon LaRouche has had to do it his whole life. And now, the enemies of the republic are at the end of their strength, and if we act in the right way now, they're going to lose. The question is, do we all go down with them, or do we save something we would call a human future, in contrast to this barbaric dark age that will be the only thing to follow, without us?

The Wellsprings of Inspiration

So, I want to give you a sense of three things about Lincoln: the sources of his own inspiration, in this American Intellectual Tradition, as we call it; his personal sense of mission; and then one of the best kept secrets, which is that he personally organized the Union Army to win the Civil War.

First, to find out about what inspired him, we must travel back to the year 1838. It was then that he made an address to the Young Men's Lyceum of Springfield, Illinois on the subject of "the perpetuation of our political institutions." At the time of Lincoln's address much had already happened since those political institutions were founded in the wake of the American Revolution. Lincoln was worried that the living memory of the American Revolution, which had sustained so many Americans, was almost gone, and that the new generation was unprepared to face the mounting threats. In his 1838 speech, he asked:

> At what point shall we expect the approach of danger? By what means shall we fortify against it? Shall we expect some trans-Atlantic military giant to step the ocean and crush us at a blow? Never! All the armies of Europe, Asia, and Africa combined, with all the treasure of the earth (our own excepted) in their military chest, with a Bonaparte for a commander, could not by force take a drink from the Ohio or make a track on the Blue Ridge in a trial of a thousand years. At what point then, is the approach of danger to be expected? I answer, If it ever reach us it must

spring up amongst us; it cannot come from abroad. If destruction be our lot we must ourselves be its author and finisher. As a nation of freemen we must live through all time, or die by suicide.

The danger is, he says, that the Revolutionary War generation is almost gone, and the memories of that struggle "can't be so universally known, and so vividly felt, as they were heretofore. At the close of that struggle, nearly every adult male had been a participator in some of its scenes. The consequence was that of those scenes—in the form of a husband, a father, a son, or a brother—a living history was to be found in every family.... But those histories are gone. They can be read no more, forever. They were a fortress of strength, but what invading foemen could not do, the silent artillery of time has done, the leveling of its walls—they're gone." The challenge Lincoln then puts forth to this audience is that they have to re-create, themselves, the means to sustain these higher principles for which so many gave their lives. He says, "Let those materials be moulded into general intelligence, sound morality, and in particular, a reverence for the Constitution and laws.... Upon these let the proud fabric of freedom rest, as the rock of its basis; and as truly as has been said of the only greater institution, the gates of hell shall not prevail against it.'"

Years later, on his way to his inauguration as President in 1861, Lincoln stopped to address the New Jersey Legislature at Trenton, a city which held special meaning for him. He told them that in "the earliest days of my being able to read, I got hold of a small book, such a one as few of the younger members have ever seen, Weem's *Life of Washington*. I remember all the accounts there given of the battlefields and struggles for the liberties of the country, and none fixed themselves upon my imagination so deeply as the struggle here at Trenton, New Jersey. The crossing of the river; the contest with the Hessians; the great hardships endured at that time, all fixed themselves on my

"Washington Crossing the Delaware," by Emanuel Leutze.

memory more than any single revolutionary event.... I recollect thinking then, boy even though I was, that there must have been something more than common that those men struggled for. I am exceedingly anxious that that thing which they struggled for; that something even more than National Independence; that something that held out a great promise to all the people of the world to all time to come: I am exceedingly anxious that this Union, the Constitution, and the liberties of the people shall be perpetuated in accordance with the original idea for which that struggle was made, and I shall be most happy indeed if I shall be an humble instrument in the hands of the Almighty, and of this, his almost chosen people, for perpetuating the object of that great struggle."

What Lincoln liked most about George Washington was that Washington would do the impossible. When it looked like the Continental Army was totally lost—had no chance at all—he said, "What don't they think we can do? We'll go do it." And that was how we attacked Trenton on Christmas Day, coming across the icy Delaware in shallow-draft boats, and surprising the whole drunken Hessian mercenary encampment. Then, Washington withdrew silently at night from right in front of a large British Army come to trap him, and captured Princeton. At the beginning of the campaign, the British held all of New Jersey, but after two such battles, they withdrew from the entire state into the "safety" of disease-infested New York City! Lincoln knew that Washington was someone to emulate and trust.

Lincoln's Sense of Mission

"I now leave, not knowing when, or whether ever, I may return, with a task before me greater than that which rested upon Washington," said Lincoln in his farewell address to his friends and neighbors in Springfield as he left for his inauguration. "Without the assistance of that Divine Being, who ever attended him, I cannot succeed. With that assistance I cannot fail. Trusting in Him, who can go with me, and remain with you, and be everywhere for good, let us confidently hope that all will yet be well."

Yet even as he boarded the train, American intelligence agents were discovering a wide-ranging plot to assassinate him and take over the government. Since Lincoln's 1838 speech, an even more outrageous group of traitors had occupied the Presidential office, culminating in James Buchanan. Buchanan had been the American minister to the Court of St. James, and had fallen right in with the British plans for a slave empire by signing the Ostend Manifesto, which called for the occupation of Cuba and the extension of slavery. Once the slave-holding states saw that Lincoln had been

President James Buchanan

elected, they started to secede, but President Buchanan made no attempt to keep them from seizing all the Federal property they could get their hands on, including arsenals, forts, Navy yards and ships, and Federal buildings of all descriptions. Not content with that, Buchanan's Cabinet members openly spoke of how to keep Lincoln from being inaugurated, while the official government newspaper, subsidized by the Administration, called for the "insulted" slave-owners to secede!

Buchanan's message to Congress on Dec. 4, 1860, presented a government in willful paralysis. Secession, he said, was unconstitutional, but there was no power in Congress or the Executive to compel a state to remain in the Union. It was the duty of the President to enforce the laws, but in the existing situation it was utterly impossible for him to do so. "The fact is," Buchanan wrote, "that our Union rests upon public opinion, and can never be cemented by the blood of its citizens shed in civil war." Earlier that year Buchanan had hosted an "unofficial" visit by the British Prince of Wales, the future Edward VII, and his large party of lordly advisors. These British

---

Lincoln on Slavery: The Dred Scott Decision

In 1857, the U.S. Supreme Court passed its infamous Dred Scott *decision, allowing a slaveholder to cross state lines, into a free state, to reclaim his "property"— a former slave who had gained his freedom. Chief Justice Roger Taney wrote in his opinion on the case, that the Declaration of Independence did not apply to the Negroes, who "had no rights that the white man was bound to respect."*

Lincoln, in a speech in Springfield, Illinois, on June 26, 1857, had this to say on the matter:

In those days [of the American Revolution], our Declaration of Independence was held sacred by all, and thought to include all; but now, to aid in making the bondage of the Negro universal and eternal, it is assailed, and sneered at, and construed, and hawked at, and torn till, if its framers could rise from their graves, they could not at all recognize it. All the powers of earth seem rapidly combining against him. Mammon is after him; ambition follows, and philosophy follows, and the Theology of the day is fast joining the cry. They have him in his prison house; they have searched his person, and left no prying instrument with him. One after another they have closed the heavy iron doors upon him, and now they have him, as it were, bolted in with a lock of a hundred keys, which can never be unlocked without the concurrence of every key; the keys in the hands of a hundred different men, and they scattered to a hundred different and distant places; and they stand musing as to what invention, in all the dominions of mind and matter, can be produced to make the impossibility of his escape more complete than it is.

---

peers met with secessionist leaders as Edward made a triumphal tour of the South, and stayed not only for the American Presidential Election, but tarried on and on, supposedly while their ship underwent repairs, in order to monitor the various plans for a *coup d'état*.

When Lincoln's inaugural train reached Philadelphia, he was told of the assassination plot against him in Baltimore, where European Mazzinians had combined with Secessionists to plan an attack as he rode through the city. Yet in his speech at Independence Hall the next day, Lincoln did not waver:

I have often inquired of myself, what great principle or idea it was that kept this confederacy [union of states—ed.] so long together. It was not the mere matter of the separation of the colonies from the mother land; but something in that

---

On the Declaration of Independence

Lincoln's speech in Springfield, Illinois, on June 26, 1856, addressed the intent of the Founding Fathers, in including in the Declaration of Independence the phrase, "all men are created equal":

They meant to set up a standard maxim for free society, which should be familiar to all, and revered by all; constantly looked to, constantly labored for, and even though never perfectly attained, constantly approximated, and thereby constantly spreading and deepening its influence, and augmenting the happiness and value of life to all peoples of all colors everywhere. The assertion that "all men are created equal" was of no practical use in effecting our separation from Great Britain; and it was placed in the Declaration, not for that, but for future use. Its authors meant it to be—thank God, it is now proving itself—a stumbling block to those who in after times might seek to turn a free people back into the hateful paths of despotism. They knew the proneness of prosperity to breed tyrants, and they meant when such should re-appear in this fair land and commence their vocation, they should find left for them at least one hard nut to crack.

Declaration giving liberty, not alone to the people of this country, but hope to the world for all future time. It was that which gave promise that in due time the weights should be lifted from the shoulders of all men, and that all should have an equal chance. This is the sentiment embodied in that Declaration of Independence.

Now, my friends, can this country be saved upon that basis? If it can, I will consider myself one of the happiest men in the world if I can help to save it. If it can't be saved upon that principle, it will be truly awful. But, if this country cannot be saved without giving up that principle—I was about to say I would rather be assassinated on this spot than to surrender it.

Now, this is someone you can look at and say, "I think this man means what he says. I think we'd better follow him, because nobody else has a clue about what we are going to do."

The situation was indeed dire—almost the entire South was seceding in open declaration of war against the United States, armed to the teeth, bankrolled to the maximum that the coffers would bear, by Britain. If you ever get a chance to tour West Point, go to what they call Trophy Point, overlooking that wide expanse of the Hudson, and there you may see a row of gleaming cannons from the Civil War, and on every single one of them is stamped "Made in Birmingham" or "Made in Manchester." They're all British-made cannons, that were captured from the Confederates during Union victories.

Lincoln talked about his mission, and the mission of the nation, in his address to Congress on Dec. 1, 1862. He said,

Fellow citizens, we cannot escape history. We of this Congress and this Administration, will be remembered in spite of ourselves. No personal significance, or insignificance, can spare one or another of us. The fiery trial through which we pass, will light us down, in honor or dishonor, to the latest generation. We say we are for the Union. The world will not forget that we say this. We know how to save the Union. The world knows we do know how to save it. We—even we here—hold the power, and bear the responsibility. In giving freedom to the slave, we assure freedom to the free—honorable alike in what we give, and what we preserve. We shall nobly save, or meanly lose, the last best hope of earth. Other means may succeed; this could not fail. The way is plain, peaceful, generous, just—a way which, if followed, the world will forever applaud, and God must forever bless.

Lincoln, the People, and the Army

Lincoln has to rally the American people, but he has to do it in a very specific way. He has to establish an understanding in the people, that when you are fighting to preserve the union, you are fighting for yourself; you're fighting so that you may have a future. Secondly, Lincoln has to somehow, personally, organize the Union Army. And he has to organize the people and the Army, together, in such a way that they are able to understand that he is the personal, living embodiment of everything that they cherish, or should cherish, and could come to cherish, about this country, about this human purpose. Now, as long as he is traveling through the country on his way to the inauguration, he is able to speak to thousands of people about what they must do. At Indianapolis, he says,

To the salvation of this Union there needs but one single thing—the hearts of a people like yours. When the people rise in masses in behalf of the Union and the liberties of their country, truly may it be said, "The gates of hell shall not prevail against them."

In all the trying positions in which I shall be placed—and doubtless I shall be placed in many trying ones—my reliance will be placed upon you and the people of the United States—and I wish you to remember now and forever, that it is your business, and not mine; that if the union of these States, and the liberties of this people, shall be lost, it is but little to any one man of 52 years of age, but a great deal to the 30 millions of people who inhabit these United States, and to their posterity in all coming time.... I, as already intimated, am but an accidental instrument, temporary, and to serve but for a limited time, but I appeal to you again to constantly bear in mind that with you, and not with politicians, not with Presidents, not with office-seekers, but with you, is the question, "Shall the Union and shall the liberties of this country be preserved to the latest generation?"

Once in Washington, and under war conditions, Lincoln rarely spoke to large audiences. But there was a way to organize the Army, and, through them, the civilians as well. How? Well, every Army unit that was not meant for the western theater of operations reported to Washington, D.C. to be trained. Lincoln made sure that he greeted every unit as it paraded by the White House, and sometimes he was able to speak at length with them. The White House itself was open to all, and many a soldier sat himself down in a chair or at a desk and wrote a letter home. Civilians, too, flocked to talk to the President, whether asking for a job or a pardon for a deserter. Often, Lincoln would delay talking to his Cabinet in order to speak to the citizens who flooded his office.

Sometimes, the President would become impatient when a new unit was scheduled to arrive by boat up the Potomac, and he would commandeer a vessel to go and meet them before they would even land. By the end of June in 1861, Lincoln had already been seen by tens of thousands of arriving soldiers in the Union Army. Many of them were young—born in the 1840s—and had had precious little to value about their government leaders. The enlisted soldiers called themselves "the boys," and their officers were "the men." Lincoln did more than just talk about the Union cause: He promoted the hospitals and medical care they would need, visited them in their encampments, and came to see them after their battles. He also went out of his way to include [in the Army] as many elements of society as possible, including the foreign-born and men from the slave states. He also stretched or cut red tape in order to form an army as soon as possible—perhaps to convince the Confederates to turn from their course. "We are in no condition to waste time on technicalities. The enthusiastic uprising of the people in our cause, is our great reliance; and we cannot safely give it any check, even though it overflows and runs in channels not laid down in any chart."

After the terrible Union defeat at Bull Run on July 21, 1861, when the picnicking Congressmen who had come to watch the battle turned tail and fled back to Washington, Lincoln got in a carriage and went from camp to camp, making short speeches of gratitude and hope. A Wisconsin soldier, Robert Beecham, wrote home that, "There was stamped on his face a fresh, vigorous, healthy and courageous look that inspired confidence. We certainly needed some encouragement. It was good to be impressed with the fact that the President on whose shoulders rested this mighty burden of war, with its vast train of results, either for weal or for woe to the people of a hemisphere, was not discouraged with the outlook." Beecham wrote that when Lincoln spoke, "he only said in a mild, gentle way, that he had confidence in the ability and patriotism of the American people and their volunteer army to meet and overcome every enemy of the republic."

When Lincoln stopped speaking, the soldiers rushed his carriage, each one wanting to shake his hand. Beecham tried to reach him, but finally gave up. "I felt like shaking hands with Mr. Lincoln myself," he wrote, "but on second thought it seemed best not to assist in wearing the poor man's life out."

Gen. George B. McClellan

The Commander-in-Chief Takes Norfolk

Gen. George McClellan, the commander of the Union forces at the beginning of the war, was an excellent drillmaster for the troops, but he seemed almost completely incapable of moving those troops in the direction of the enemy. He finally floated the Army of the Potomac down to the Peninsula of Virginia, but there he sat, immoveable, while he demanded 100,000 more men, and then another 100,000. His dispatches to Lincoln complained constantly about the weather, the mud, the overpowering numbers of the Confederate Army, and his manpower weakness. At first, Lincoln tried humor. He said that McClellan was an admirable engineer, "but he seems to have a special talent for the stationary engine." One day, someone called on Lincoln and stated that he had a family problem. His sick relative lived in Richmond, and he asked for a pass that would take him behind the enemy lines. Lincoln asked, "Are you going to really use the pass?" "Of course, Mr. President." "Because I gave George McClellan 125,000 passes' to Richmond and he still hasn't used them." Finally, Lincoln sent General McClellan a note saying, "My dear McClellan, If you don't want to use the Army, I should like to borrow it for a while."

At this time, Lincoln had no replacement for McClellan, so he didn't want to fire him. One day in 1862, Senator Wade from Ohio came to the White House and demanded that Lincoln immediately fire General McClellan. Lincoln answered, "Senator, who would you put in McClellan's place?" "Anybody," snorted Wade. "Wade," replied Lincoln, "anybody will do for you, but I must have somebody." It was at this time that Lincoln started to borrow books on military theory from the Library of Congress. He also began an almost daily inspection of new weapons systems, and he was especially interested in the design and construction of the Union ironclad, the *Monitor*.

In May 1862, with McClellan still sitting on the Peninsula and making no move toward Richmond, Lincoln took Secretary of War Stanton and Secretary of the Treasury Chase with him down to Hampton Roads, Virginia. McClellan sent word that he was "too busy" to see his Commander-in-Chief, so Lincoln inspected the *Monitor* and decided to embark on a campaign of his own—to the delight of the soldiers and sailors. Although Fort Monroe had been successfully held for the Union by Gen. John Wool, and the Union Navy filled Hampton Roads with ships, the Confederates still held the town and Navy yard of Norfolk.

Since the famous battle two months before between the *Monitor* and the Confederate ironclad *Merrimac*, the *Merrimac* had been lurking at Norfolk, threatening the Union ships. Lincoln proposed that the Navy ferry a contingent of Union troops over to Norfolk in order to capture the town. Naval officers protested, however, that the shallow water would not allow them to get within a mile of the shore.

Lincoln, who in his youth had twice helped steer a flatboat down the treacherous Mississippi from Illinois to New Orleans, carefully studied a map of Hampton Roads. He consulted with General Wool, a 78-year-old veteran of the War of 1812 who was still full of fight, and he approved the plan. So on the night of May 10, Lincoln and two Cabinet secretaries pulled away for Norfolk in a small boat to the spot that Lincoln had

Lincoln with his Army at Antietam on Oct. 3, 1862 (Gen. George McClellan is facing off against him).

chosen. The water, indeed, was deep enough, and Lincoln jumped ashore and took a walk on enemy territory. Lincoln reported his findings, and General Wool's troops went ashore the next day only to find that the Confederates had gotten wind of Lincoln's maneuver and had abandoned the city! All they saw was the Mayor of Norfolk walking toward them holding out the keys to the city. Left without a base, the crew of the dreaded *Merrimac* blew her up and fled.

"So ended a brilliant week's campaign by the President," recorded Treasury Secretary Chase, "for I think it quite certain that if he had not gone down, Norfolk would still have been in the possession of the enemy, and the *Merrimac* as grim and defiant as ever." The headlines in the New York newspapers hailed "President Lincoln's First Military and Naval Operation—Its Great Success."

The episode made a considerable impression on the men at Fort Monroe. A soldier wrote of seeing "Mr. Lincoln driving past to take possession of Norfolk." "It is extremely fortunate that the President came down as he did," wrote an officer of the *Monitor* that day; "he seems to have infused new life into everything." In what had been a scene of inactivity, he saw Lincoln "stirring up the dry bones."

Still unable to see General McClellan, Private Lincoln boarded a steamer up the Chesapeake, standing on the deck with his hat off, bowing to the cheering sailors on the *Monitor* and the other Navy vessels that he passed.

Nine days later, Lincoln quietly signed the Homestead Act into law. Vetoed by President Buchanan in 1860, the law provided for the transfer of 160 acres of unoccupied public land to each homesteader for a nominal fee, if he and his family lived there and worked the land for five years. Even while the Civil War continued to rage, thousands of pioneers were flooding west across the Mississippi, fulfilling Lincoln's vision for the peace which was to come.

'We're Coming, Father Abraham'

General McClellan eventually moved the Army to Maryland, where one of the bloodiest battles of the war was fought at Antietam Creek, on Sept. 17, 1862. Confederate commander Gen. Robert E. Lee had moved his Army into Maryland, and McClellan had fortuitously captured his plans, but McClellan threw away his advantage by poor planning, and turned the battle into a bloodbath by insisting on sending wave after wave of Union troops over a narrow bridge, with Confederate cannons before them and Confederate sharpshooters above them. Lee and his men escaped across the Potomac, because McClellan ignored Lincoln's orders to pursue and cut off the Potomac crossings. Lincoln was bitter about the unnecessary bloodshed, and he was furious when he received information about a court martial being conducted of a certain Maj. John Key. Asked why McClellan did not go after Lee and crush him, Key had replied, "That is not the game." Instead, he said, the intent in the Army was merely "that neither army shall get much advantage of the other; that both shall be kept in the field till they are exhausted, when we will make a compromise and save slavery."

Lincoln insisted on questioning the man himself, and the officer repeated the same viewpoint to the President. "If there was a game' ever among Union men, to have our Army not take an advantage of the enemy when it could," Lincoln said, then he was going "to break up that game." He determined to go once more to the Army in person. Lincoln counted those present for duty at over 88,000, even after the recent losses, but there they sat on the fields around McClellan's tent. That night he climbed a ridge with his friend Ozias Hatch, and asked Hatch what he saw. "The Army of the Potomac," he replied; but Lincoln retorted, "So it is called, but that is a mistake; it is only McClellan's bodyguard."

President Lincoln took part in a review of McClellan's troops on October 3, and many of the soldiers present recorded their impressions of him on that day. "Mr. Lincoln was manifestly touched," observed an officer in the 6th Wisconsin, "and he, himself, looked serious and careworn." Lincoln kept bowing low in response to the salutes from the ragged banners, but some of the soldiers felt their hearts going out to him, instead. "How the smile from a care-worn and anxious face touched the hearts of those bronzed, rough-looking men," wrote another. Almost every soldier who kept a diary or wrote a letter home after the review made some mention of his own sight of the President. One soldier of the newly dubbed Iron Brigade of Wisconsin said, "Altogether he is the man to suit the soldiers." And now, for the first time, the soldiers begin to refer to Lincoln as "Father Abraham."

When Lincoln arrived in Gettysburg the night before he delivered his immortal address, throngs of soldiers and citizens filled the streets singing, "We Are Coming, Father Abraham" until one in the morning. In 1864, General McClellan, now relieved of command, was to be the Democratic candidate for the Presidency against Lincoln. Lincoln was, as the soldiers had written, very "care-worn," but he had to run again. Henry Wing was a young reporter for the *New York Tribune* who covered the war at the front, and whenever he returned to Washington, Lincoln wanted him to come see him and "tell me all you hear and see." On one of these visits before the 1864 election, Lincoln said, "There's many a night, Henry, that I plan to resign. I wouldn't run again now if

Lincoln and McClellan at Antietam on Oct. 3, 1862. McClellan was relieved of command shortly thereafter, and became, in 1864, the Democratic Party candidate for President.

I didn't know these other fellows couldn't save the Union on their platforms, whatever they say. I can't quit, Henry. I have to stay."

In August of that election year, Lincoln addressed the 166th Ohio Infantry Regiment when it returned from the front:

It is not merely for today, but for all time to come that we should perpetuate for our children's children this great and free government, which we have enjoyed all our lives. I beg you to remember this, not merely for my sake, but for yours. I happen temporarily to occupy this big White House. I am a living witness that any one of your children may look to come here as my father's child has. It is in order that each of you may have, through this free government which we have enjoyed, an open field and a fair chance for your industry, enterprise and intelligence; that you may all have equal privileges in the race of life,

Some of the 4,300 supply wagons that followed the Union Army as it moved south to The Wilderness battlefield in Virginia, May 1864.

with all its desirable human aspirations. It is for this the struggle should be maintained, that we may not lose our birthright—not only for one, but for two or three years. The nation is worth fighting for, to secure such an inestimable jewel.

There was jubilation over Lincoln's defeat of McClellan in the 1864 election. The Army had voted for Lincoln by an overwhelming margin of better than two to one. Now, among the soldiers, he was almost universally referred to as "Father Abraham." But, there was also another note. The men saw in the President's victory what a Pennsylvania artilleryman regarded as an assurance that "the sacrifices that the soldier has made, have not been in vain, and that the war will continue until the parties who brought our present National troubles upon us, will be compelled to submit to the law and the cause of our troubles removed forever." And not for the first time, the soldiers compared Lincoln to another President. "Future history will place Mr. Lincoln's name next to Washington," a Pennsylvania volunteer said two weeks after the election. "The first the founder, the second the preserver of our country."

Richmond, At Last

In late March 1865, Lincoln steamed down to Fort Monroe and then up the James River to his Army's headquarters at City Point. He wanted to spend all of the final days of the war with the Army. Then news came that Lee had marched out of Richmond, and Union General Weitzel was marching in to take possession of the Confederate capital. "Thank God," said Lincoln, fervently, "that I have lived to see this! It seems to me that I have been dreaming a horrid dream for four years, and now the nightmare is gone. I want to see Richmond." Adm. David Porter, a supporter of General McClellan and not a warm friend of the President, wrote an account of Lincoln's journey. Lincoln was warned that there might still be Confederate troops or sharpshooters in the area; there were fires still burning, and no one knew exactly what the situation in the city was. But he was adamant, and after the channel was cleared of torpedoes, a flotilla of boats set off up the James River. All were jockeying in order to be the first one into the city, but all were grounded one after the other. Admiral Porter took Lincoln and his young son Tad onto his barge, and, with a small number of marines, they beat everyone to the city.

As Lincoln stepped onto land, holding the hand of his son, a small group of Negroes digging with spades recognized him from a picture which they had kept for four years. They fell on their knees before him, but Lincoln, embarrassed, said, "Don't kneel to me. That is not right, You must kneel to God only, and thank him for the liberty you will hereafter enjoy. I am but God's humble instrument; but you may rest assured that as long as I live no one shall put a shackle to your limbs and you shall have all the rights which God has given to every other free citizen of this Republic." Porter said that as Lincoln said this, although he was not a handsome man, and ungainly in his person, "yet in his enthusiasm he seemed the personification of manly beauty." Porter realized they had to move on, and asked the patriarch of the group to withdraw and let them pass. The now ex-slaves joined hands in a circle and sang a hymn, and as they did so, the formerly deserted streets were

Lincoln entering Richmond, April 4, 1865.

now filled with ex-slaves, all joyously trying to get a glimpse of Lincoln.

Porter reported that the crowd could not be made to understand that they were detaining the President, for "they looked upon him as belonging to them, and that he had come to put the crowning act to the great work he had commenced. They would not feel that they were free in reality until they heard it from his own lips." Lincoln spoke again: "My poor friends, you are free—free as air. You can cast off the name of slave and trample upon it; it will come to you no more. Liberty is your birthright. God gave it to you as he gave it to others, and it is a sin that you have been deprived of it for so many years. But you must try to deserve this priceless boon." (This was the same thing he had told those young men in Springfield, 27 years before.) "Let the world see that you merit it, and are able to maintain it by your good works. Don't let your joy carry you into excesses. Learn the laws and obey them; obey God's commandments and thank him for giving you liberty, for to him you owe all things. There, now, let me pass on; I have but little time to spare. I want to see the capital, and must return at once to Washington to secure to you that liberty which you seem to prize so highly...."

Winning the Political Fight Today

If you think of the way that Lincoln set out, you see that he defined the problem in the only way you can define it: We're not trying to defeat the enemy because they're evil. I have to do this because the posterity of all time to come depends on it. Everyone who has gotten us this far—the Founding Fathers, the Nathaniel Greenes, the Robert Fultons, you name them, the Daniel Boones, the Benjamin Franklins, every one of them—if we do not win, we will effectively deny their existence; we take away their posterity. Whether you know it or not, you are already part of a mission to do the greatest good, perpetuate the greatest good that's ever been done in the history of the human race. And if that statement is too big for you, then you do have to study more American history, and you'll see that it's true. That is an *ironclad* truth. And the way you get at it is not to find out the whos and whats and the years, and the these and the those and the thems. You have to start to say: "Wait a minute, I can get inside the mind of this person; I can re-experience how they solved a problem." What makes you human is the ability to re-create in your own mind, the greatest creative output of the greatest minds in any period of history. What you find is happening, is that these people become so familiar to you that they are your friends! You've got em. They're there to rely on.

Then when you read something by Lincoln, you don't just say, "Those are nice words. What a great idea. Nice poetry!" No, you start to look at his mind and say, "Look what this man pulled in, in terms of the significance of his life, and carried it to the limit of anything you could imagine." But to him, that is what he was; that was who he was; normal; that was human. That was his mission; his mission was to become a true human being.

So Lincoln typifies, at the highest level, somebody who could get this through to other people; so that he created, or he improved, a lot of really wonderful people. There are a lot of other friends out there, waiting. You've got to bring them back into the war. And if we get them back into the war, the way Lincoln did—and we won the Civil War because Lincoln did that—then we will win this war too. There's no other way to do it.

In the Garden of Gethsemane

by Lyndon H. LaRouche, Jr.

A prophet is not without honor, save in his own country.

—Matthew 13:57

Those of us who find ourselves in Gethsemane—a Gethsemane where we are told that we must take a role of leadership with our eye on Christ on the Cross-often experience something which, unfortunately, most people do not. We tend to look at things from a different standpoint. Before trying to situate how I see the recent period, and the period immediately before us, I should try to communicate what my viewpoint is, a viewpoint which I know is shared in some degree of very close approximation by everyone who has gone to Gethsemane with the view of the Cross in his eyes, saying, "He did it, I am now being told that I must, too, walk in His way."

What I suggest often, in trying to explain this to a person who has not experienced it, is to say: "Imagine a time 50 years after you're dead. Imagine in that moment, 50 years ahead, that you can become conscious and look back at the entirety of your mortal life, from its beginning to its ending. And, rather than seeing that mortal life as a succession of experiences, you see it as a unity. Imagine facing the question respecting that mortal life, asking, "Was that life necessary in the total scheme of the universe and the existence of mankind, was it necessary that I be born in order to lead that life, the sum total of that number of years between birth and death? Did I do something, or did my living represent something, which was positively beneficial to present generations, and implicitly to future generations after me? If so, then I should have walked through that life with joy, knowing that every moment was precious to all mankind, because what I was doing by living was something that was needed by all mankind, something beneficial to all mankind."

If I am wise, then 50 years after my death, in looking back at my mortal life, I know that from the beginning with my birth, to the end with my death, that my truest self-interest was the preservation and enhancement of that which made my having lived important to those around me and those who came after me.

That is the beginning, I think, of true wisdom; that is the beginning of the Passion, which sometimes enables each of us when called to walk through our own peculiar kind of Gethsemane. It is from this standpoint, that the mind of an individual such as our own, can efficiently comprehend history in the large.

A second point, which I often raise, I think is essential to understand the few simple observations I have to make here. It is that, in human reason, in the power, for example, to effect a valid, fundamental scientific discovery, which overturns, in large degree, previous scientific opinion, we see a fundamental distinction between man and all beasts. This power of creative reason, typified by the power to make a valid, fundamental scientific discovery, and also the power to transmit and to receive such a discovery, is that which sets man apart from and above the beasts.

The emotion associated with that kind of human activity, whether in physical science, in the development of creative works or performance of creative works of classical culture or simply in the caring for a child to nurture that quality of potential for discovery in the child, is true love. Creative activity is human activity, and the emotion associated with that kind of activity, is true love.

We start from that and say that society must be based on these considerations, that. every human being, being apart from and above the animals, has the right and the obligation to live an important life. Every human being has the right to do something, such that if one looked back 50 years after the death of that person at his or her

Lyndon H. LaRouche, Jr.

whole mortal life, one could have said, that life was necessary to all humanity. At the same time, one could distinguish some use of this creative power of reasoning as the activity which made that life important, simply, sometimes, the development of that creative power.

We have, in the entirety of the approximately 2,500 years of Western European history, which includes the history of the Americas, two conflicting views of mankind. One view shares more or less the standpoint I've just identified: We view the human individual as bearing the divine spark of potential for reason, as a sacred life; a spark of reason which must be developed by society, nurtured by society, given opportunity for fruitful expression by society; a quality of activity whose good works must be adopted by society, protected by society, and preserved by society, for the benefit of present and future generations. That is the republic, the republic as conceived by Solon's constitution of Athens-a notion of republic, which, in our time, is made nobler by the Christian understanding, which transforms and elevates the contributions of Solon and Socrates after him.

On the other side, there is the conception of Sparta, a privileged oligarchy, brutalizing the Helots, the slaves, the so-called lower classes. That, too is a model society, not a republic, but an oligarchy.

The struggle between these two views of mankind is epitomized by the struggle between President and General George Washington, on the one side, and King George III on the other. George Washington was a soldier and statesman of the republic, not a perfect one, but a good one. On the opposite side was poor King George III, the puppet of the evil Earl of Shelbourne, and the epitome of oligarchism, the heritage of Sparta. The tradition of King George III, which deems that some men must be kept slaves, is an oligarchical view, which hates the idea of the equality of the individual in respect to the individual human being's possession of that divine spark, the individual human being's right to the development of that spark, the nurture of its activity, and the defense and perpetuation of its good works.

Such is the conflict. In our time, the great American Republic, by virtue of the cultivation of ignorance and concern with smallness of mind, and neglect of the importance of what comes after us in the living of our mortal lives, has been so undermined, degraded, and corrupted, that we as a nation no longer are the nation we were conceived to be, but instead have become a nation brain-drained in front of our television sets, thinking with greater passion about mere spectator sports or mere television soap-opera than we do about urgent events in real life. We are a nation seeking gratification in drugs, in sordid forms of sexual activity, in other sordid entertainments, in that kind of pleasure-seeking, which echoes the words *Sodom and Gomorrah*.

And so, oligarchism, that which George III of England represented back in the eighteenth century, has taken over and rules the land which was once George Washington's.

What this leads to is this. Today, there is a great revolution around the world against tyranny in all forms. So far, this revolution has manifested itself within the communist sector against communist tyrannies. But it is coming here, too. Wherever the divine spark of reason is being crushed by oligarchical regimes, with all their cruelties, the divine spark of reason within human beings inspires them to arise, to throw off the tyranny-not out of anger and rage against tyranny, but because the divine spark of reason in each person *must* be *affirmed*. We seek not merely to be free from oligarchy; we seek to be free from oligarchy, because not to do so would be to betray the divine spark of reason in ourselves and in others.

The secret of great revolutions, of great civil rights movements, as Dr. King's example illustrates, is this capacity, which the Greek New Testament called *agapē*, which Latin called *caritas*, which the King James version of the Bible calls *charity*, which we otherwise know as *love*. Whenever this power of love, this recognition of that divine spark, setting us above the beasts, prevails, wherever people can approximate that view of the sum total of their lives, as if from 50 years after their deaths, whenever movements arise which, out of love, produce people who are willing, not fruitlessly, but for a purpose, to *lay down their lives*, so that their lives might have greater meaning, for this purpose-there you have the great revolutions of history.

If we were to project events on the basis of what is taught in the schools about revolutions and other struggles of the past, then the human race at present were doomed. If we say that people struggle against this and that oppression, and so forth, and out of rage or whatnot, overthrow their cruel oppressor, we should lose; the human race would lose. However, if we touch the force of love, the spark of divine reason, we unleash a force, a creative force, a divine force, which is greater than any adversary, and we win. Those revolutions, which are based upon the appeal to this divine spark of reason within the individual, prevailed. Those which worked otherwise produced abominations, or simply failed.

Yes, we must struggle against injustice. But it is not enough to struggle out of anger. We must struggle out of love. And that we learn best, who have had to walk as leaders of one degree or another, through our own Gethsemane, with the image of the Cross before us.

That is the best I can say. I might say it better, but what I try to say with these poor words, is the best I can say summarily, on the subject of current history. I believe, that the great upsurge of humanity, implicit in the optimism I express, is now in progress. I am persuaded that we shall win, provided that each of us can find in ourselves, that which makes us the right arm of the Creator, a man, a woman of providence, within the limits of our own capacities and opportunities.

Lyndon H. LaRouche, Jr.
Dictated from prison
Rochester, Minnesota
January 17, 1990

FIDELIO

Journal of Poetry, Science, and Statecraft

From the first issue, dated Winter 1992, featuring Lyndon LaRouche on "The Science of Music: The Solution to Plato's Paradox of 'The One and the Many,'" to the final issue of Spring/Summer 2006, a "Symposium on Edgar Allan Poe and the Spirit of the American Revolution," *Fidelio* magazine gave voice to the Schiller Institute's intention to create a new Golden Renaissance.

The title of the magazine, is taken from Beethoven's great opera, which celebrates the struggle for political freedom over tyranny. *Fidelio* was founded at the time that LaRouche and several of his close associates were unjustly imprisoned, as was the opera's Florestan, whose character was based on the American Revolutionary hero, the French General, Marquis de Lafayette.

Each issue of *Fidelio*, throughout its 14-year lifespan, remained faithful to its initial commitment, and offered original writings by LaRouche and his associates, on matters of, what the poet Percy Byssche Shelley identified as, "profound and impassioned conceptions respecting man and nature."

Back issues are now available for purchase through the Schiller Institute website:
http://schillerinstitute.org/about/order_form.html

Failure of Leadership Caused Hurricane Harvey Disaster

by Evelyn Lantz

Sept. 6—The disaster which all of us in Houston and in large parts of Texas and Louisiana lived through, and are still living through, was not the result of a natural disaster. It was because the quality of leadership which Lyndon and Helga LaRouche and the LaRouche movement represent, was not heeded.

The headline on the *Hamiltonian* which we are distributing in New York and Houston—"Wall Street Created Hurricane Harvey Castastrophe"—is right.

My husband, Brian Lantz, pointed out an article in the *Dallas Morning News* which quoted Harris County's former flood control director, Arthur Storey. Although this man probably saved my house and the houses of many of the members of the LaRouche movement in this area of Houston because of his flood control work in the 1990's, he courageously admitted in the article that he had failed to do what was necessary.

The story reports on a proposal from the 1990's to build a channel under the freeway to carry off floodwater which was too much to be handled by the Buffalo Bayou alone—a channel which was never built! Many of the homes in west Houston which are now being flooded, would not have been flooded if this project had been built twenty years ago.

The article quoted Arthor Storey saying, "My embarrassment was that I knew this was going to happen. And I was not smart enough, or bold enough, to fight the system, to fight the politics and stop it."

If we are to change our policies so that this kind of catastrophe does not continue to happen, we require the leadership which *is* smart enough and bold enough. This kind of thing is on people's minds now: that this was not just a "natural catastrophe"—that it didn't have to happen.

Addendum: The truth of Arthur Storey's words was underlined in two ways just this evening. First, the *Houston Chronicle* online edition carried almost the exact story which was carried in the *Dallas Morning News, except* that Mr. Storey's quote was eliminated, and the story ends with another quote which had preceded his in the original article, about how difficult it would have been to build the project.

And, as I was putting these words on paper, a story came over the local ABC news channel featuring Arthur Storey, who was being interviewed as he was working on his own home which has been flooded! He angrily told the interviewer that this is a man-made catastrophe!

Air National Guard/staff Sgt. Daniel J. Martinez

An aerial view of extensive flooding in southeast Texas, Aug. 31, 2017.

CHINA AND RUSSIA DRIVE NEW PARADIGM

BRICS Summit and Eastern Economic Forum Give Hope to Mankind

by Mike Billington

Sept. 9—Participants in the new world paradigm—including representatives of most of the human race—gathered together in two dramatic conferences during the week of September 3-8: the BRICS Summit in Xiamen, China, followed by the Eastern Economic Forum (EEF) in Vladivostok, Russia. These meetings could not have come at a more dramatic moment in history. The western financial system is facing a catastrophic collapse, exceeding by an order of magnitude the crisis which began in 2007. Faced with this looming disaster, the British empire, through its financial centers in the City of London, Wall Street, and across Europe, is resorting to extreme measures to sabotage this move by the majority of the world's nations. The Chinese and Russian-led process, in rejecting the "Washington Consensus" (better called the British Empire straight-jacket), which imposed austerity and political-economic conditionalities on supposedly sovereign states, is instead engaging in the "win-win" policies of the China-Russia New Silk Road (Belt and Road Initiative), offering nation-building through infrastructure and industrial development, without political dictates.

Perhaps even more frightening to the Lords of London and Wall Street, is the intention of President Donald Trump to join in this New Paradigm, to break

Presidents Narendra Modi, Vladimir Putin, and Xi Jinping at the BRICS Summit in Xiamen, China.

the imperial East vs. West divide in favor of friendship with Russia and China, both in combatting international terrorism and through participation in the New Silk Road—including welcoming Chinese help in rebuilding the crumbling U.S. industry and infrastructure. This is the core motivation driving the British-directed coup attempt against President Trump.

Now is the time for the American people to back President Trump's best intentions—to join in the phase shift in history demonstrated this past week in Asia. This has been the commitment of the LaRouche movement, including this journal, for the past fifty years—to bring the world together behind a "peace through de-

The 2017 BRICS Summit in Xiamen, southeast China's Fujian Province, Sept. 4, 2017.

velopment" perspective, bringing humanity out of its squabbling childhood to cooperate in building our world, and worlds beyond.

BRICS-Plus

China was the host for this year's annual BRICS Summit, its tenth, comprising Brazil, Russia, India, China and South Africa. China's President Xi Jinping, as the host, initiated a process he called BRICS-Plus, expanding the vision of BRICS-centered development by inviting five other nations representative of the developing sector in Southeast Asia, Africa, Ibero-America, Central Asia and the Mideast. (The participating countries were Thailand, Guinea, Mexico, Tajikistan, and Egypt.) At the concluding press conference of the BRICS Summit, President Xi said: "The dialogue of emerging market and developing countries hosted by China has sent a strong message for closer South-South cooperation and global development cooperation." He said the BRICS needed to reach out extensively to other countries to forge development partnerships and establish an open and diverse network of development partners.

Xi Jinping's address to the BRICS Business Forum, which included business leaders from the BRICS and 20 other countries, praised the role of the BRICS over the past ten years, which held steady against the global economic crisis unleashed by the bursting of the speculative bubble in the US and Europe in 2007-08. "In the past ten years," Xi said, "our combined GDP has grown by 179%, trade by 94%, and urban population by 28%. All this has contributed significantly to stabilizing the global economy and returning it to growth, and deliv-

ered tangible benefits to three billion and more people."

Xi also said: "Some people, seeing that emerging market and developing countries have experienced growth setbacks, assert that the BRICS countries are losing their luster. It is true that, affected by complex internal and external environments, we BRICS countries have encountered headwinds of varying intensity. But the growth potential and trend of our countries remain unchanged, and we are fully confident about it."

The BRICS mechanism is characterized, he continued, by the fact that the countries treat each other as equals and seek common ground, taking a results-oriented innovative approach to matters so that the results will benefit all—they "developed themselves to help others with the well-being of the world in mind."

He added: "BRICS is not a talking shop, but a task-force that gets things done, thus giving concrete expression to the endeavor of building a new type of international relations featuring win-win cooperation ... The Belt and Road Initiative is not a tool to advance any geopolitical agenda, but a platform for practical cooperation. It is not a foreign aid scheme, but an initiative for interconnected development which calls for extensive consultation, joint contribution and shared benefits. I am convinced that the Belt and Road Initiative will serve as a new platform for all countries to achieve win-win cooperation."

A major topic of discussion at the Summit was the functioning of the New Development Bank (NDB), the BRICS bank set up at the BRICS Summit in Brazil in 2014, which has begun lending over this past year, beginning with four infrastructure investments in Russia, China and India, totaling $1.4 billion. The first regional center of the NDB, the African Regional Center, was established in South Africa in August.

The South African Deputy Minister for International Relations, Luwellyn Landers, wrote in the Sept. 6 issue of *Voices360*: "The BRICS Bank was originally intended by the BRICS leaders to supplement the existing efforts of multilateral and regional financial institutions for global growth and development. However, the expectations for this Bank have clearly outweighed its

Chinese President Xi Jinping delivers a keynote speech at the opening ceremony of the BRICS Business Forum, Sept. 3, 2017.

modest origins, and it has now evolved to become a symbol of a new generation financial institution that will serve the developmental needs of the Global South." He noted that NDB loans will be approved in a streamlined manner, and "without setting conditionalities, as is the case in the established Western Multilateral Development Banks."

Landers continued: "The NDB comes at an opportune moment, as we transition from a unipolar world order with a declining power to a multi-polar world order, challenging the previous order's hegemon(s). The BRICS Bank therefore provides emerging markets and developing countries with an alternative global financial and institutional architecture. It also provides the global South with an amplified voice to articulate our core needs and set new agendas according to shared rule-formulation practices. To this end the NDB has indicated a number of innovative measures that will ultimately challenge the pre-eminence that the Washington Consensus has cultivated since the post-Second World War era. For example, the NDB is embarking on facilitating loans in the local currency of its members, which indirectly challenges the role of previous dominant currencies. As a result, countries requesting a loan no longer need to absorb the uncertainty inherent in fluctuations of currency in respect of their repayments. This in itself will provide new certainty for lenders as well as borrowers, indicative of the type of qualitative paradigm shift intended with these initiatives."

He added that the NDB will oversee the establish-

ment of a BRICS rating agency, to provide an alternative to the London-New York agencies Standard and Poors, Fitch, and Moody's. He noted that the NDB "will not impose its demands on the country needing assistance. This constitutes the fundamental difference between Chinese cooperation versus Official Development Assistance (ODA) from the West/OECD. The West has pursued, through its ODA programmes, a form of relationship which has been perceived as that of neo-colonialism."

Great Projects

A number of large-scale infrastructure projects were officially signed on the sidelines of the BRICS Summit, in bilateral discussions between the heads of state. Thailand's Prime Minister Prayut Chan-ocha signed a contract for China to build the first high speed railroad in the country, from Bangkok to Korat in Thailand's Northeast, which will begin construction next month. This railroad will eventually be extended to Laos, to connect with the rail line China is building through Laos, thus connecting Kunming, China, and points north, to the ports in Thailand. Prayut intends to make Korat the hub for the development of the entire Mekong River region. Ironically, Korat was the site of one of the primary U.S. airbases which rained bombs and napalm across Laos, Cambodia and Vietnam during the Indochina War, but it will now be the center of the region's development.

The Brazilian power companies Eletrobras and Eletronuclear signed an MOU with the China National Nuclear Corporation to facilitate China's assistance in completing the long-delayed 1.4 MW Angra 3 nuclear power plant, which has been repeatedly stalled since its launch in 1984, for political reasons. Unfortunately, there was no mention of the Interoceanic Rail Corridor, a railroad project traversing the South American Continent, which was agreed upon by Brazil, China and Peru at the BRICS Summit in 2014 at Fortaleza, Brazil. President Michel Temer, who replaced the deposed President Dilma Rousseff, has undermined many of the projects which she had championed.

India and China

The presence of Indian Prime Minister Narendra Modi at the BRICS Summit was a critical step forward in the sometimes contentious relations between China

kremlin.ru

Vladimir Putin addressing the Plenary Session of the Eastern Economic Forum.

and India. The military showdown which had festered for many weeks on the trilateral border of China, India and Bhutan, regarding contested sovereignty between Bhutan and China over the Doklam region, had threatened to undermine relations between the two Asian giants, and possibly prevent Modi's attendance at the Summit. (Modi had skipped the Belt and Road Forum in Beijing in May.)

But the Doklam crisis was amicably settled just days before the BRICS Summit, and Modi played an important role in the proceedings. He met for over an hour privately with Xi Jinping, and agreed to work to improve trust and cooperation between the two nations. Both pointed to the historic China-India Treaty of 1954, in which the Five Principles of Peaceful Coexistence were codified, which became the basis for the agreement among the formerly colonized nations of Asia and Africa at the Bandung Conference in Indonesia in April 1955. These principles are respect for sovereignty and territorial integrity, non-aggression, non-interference in internal affairs, equality, and peaceful coexistence.

China had not wished to include reference to the terrorist organizations which are based in Pakistan in the final communiqué, due to concern for relations with Pakistan, but ceded ground to Modi on this issue, accepting reference to Lashkar-e-Taiba (LeT) and Jaish-e-Mohammed (JeM) in the joint statement. JeM is active against India in Kashmir, while LeT operates across South Asia, and has recently organized a terrorist

operation within Myanmar among the Rohingya Muslim population. Modi visited Myanmar after the BRICS Summit, giving support to the Myanmar government in its fight against this terrorist network.

Eastern Economic Forum

Immediately following the BRICS Summit, over 3,500 people from 60 countries gathered in Vladivostok, Russia, for the third annual Eastern Economic Forum, targeting the development of the vast, resource-rich, but underdeveloped and underpopulated Russian Far East. The Russian Far East, together with the Arctic, can be considered the last New Frontier on Earth, comparable to the development of the American West during our first century as a nation.

In greetings sent to all the participants before the opening, President Vladimir Putin wrote: "Russia is faced with an ambitious target: to provide the best possible conditions for doing business in the Far East; to launch new manufacturing capabilities, and to create additional jobs.... Russia's Far Eastern strategy is based on openness to collaboration and an interest in promoting the broadest possible international cooperation. As such, the theme of working together within multilateral structures such as the Eurasian Economic Community, the Shanghai Cooperation Organization, ASEAN, and APEC, takes up, by tradition, an important part of the Forum agenda. I am confident that your discussions will facilitate the development of effective models for combining various integration processes, and will help us to move further towards creating a Greater Eurasian partnership."

Japan-Russia Cooperation: The two primary developments at the Forum were, first, Japan and South Korea's participation in the process of developing the Russian Far East; and, secondly, the interrelated issue of solving the crisis regarding North Korea.

Of the 3,500 participants in the Forum, fully 1,300 were from Japan, including Prime Minister Shinzo Abe

Russian President Vladimir Putin (right) and Japan Prime Minister Shinzo Abe at their joint press conference following their talks at the Eastern Economic Forum in Vladivostok.

and three of his ministers, and a large number of business leaders. The growing friendship between Abe and Putin was further consolidated, with concrete discussion of building a rail connection between Russia and Japan—first from the Russian mainland to Sakhalin Island, and then from Sakhalin to Japan's northern island, Hokkaido. Putin described the project as "absolutely global in nature," and suggested it could be completed within three to five years.

A Japanese economist who attended the Forum said that the Japanese business leaders were extremely enthusiastic, perceiving that the political relations between the two countries—which have never signed a peace treaty from World War II due to conflicting sovereignty claims over the four Kuril Islands (called the Northern Territories in Japan)—had so improved that they could begin to think freely of joint investment and development projects, without concern that political problems would interfere.

Russian Deputy Prime Minister Igor Shuvalov said of this Sakhalin rail project that it would "create a completely different context for the Kurils." Putin and Abe had already launched joint development projects in the Kurils. Speaking before the Forum, Abe told TASS: "President Putin visited my hometown of Nagato last December. The history of Japanese-Russian relations entered a new era at that time. Russia and Japan have made considerable progress over the past year, which we had been unable to make over the past 70 years. We should put an end to the abnormal situation when we still don't have a peace treaty." In fact, both Abe and Putin expressed confidence that they would be able to sign a peace treaty during their terms in office.

Peace and Development in Korea: The western media (and most governments) are warning that a war between the U.S. and North Korea is nearly unavoidable. This is not the view in Asia— including in South Korea. While China, Russia and South Korea have supported extremely tough sanctions on Pyongyang due to its continuing advances in missile and nuclear weapon development, they are at the same time preparing for cooperation with North Korea in fundamental infrastructure, trade and industrial development. Not only is this the only sane approach, since a war would be catastrophic for all of Asia and probably the entire world, but it also is essential to bring North Korea into the process of developing the Russian Far East and bringing all of the East Asian nations together for mutual benefit.

The new South Korean President, Moon Jae-in, held a long meeting with Vladimir Putin on the sidelines of

The world's first icebreaking liquefied natural-gas tanker will be the flagship of a 15-vessel Russian fleet for huge projects, with Chinese, French, and other partners, in the resource-rich Russian Arctic.

the Forum. Speaking to the press afterwards, the two men presented an inspiring vision, and several concrete programs, for working together towards the transformation of the Russian Far East, while creating the conditions for a solution to the escalating crisis over North Korea. This involves a development process that will include both the necessary security for all nations, together with economic development of North Korea and the region.

President Putin praised South Korea as "one of Russia's key partners in the Asia-Pacific Region," noting that bilateral trade had increased 50% over the past six months to $10 billion per annum, while more than 600 Korean companies are working in Russia. He said the two presidents have "agreed to stimulate the operation of the joint investment and finance platforms in the Far East, where we can make use of the opportunities offered by the priority development areas and the Free Port of Vladivostok." He added that the two nations will discuss a trade agreement between South Korea and the Eurasian Economic Union.

Putin noted "the potential involvement of South Korean companies in the construction of infrastructure facilities in Russia, including the modernization of Far Eastern ports and shipyards, and the joint development of the Northern Sea Route."

Most important, Putin said: "I would like to say that Russia is still willing to implement trilateral projects with the participation of North Korea. We could deliver Russian pipeline gas to Korea, and integrate the power lines and railway systems of Russia, the Republic of Korea and North Korea. The implementation of these initiatives will be not only economically beneficial, but will also help build up trust and stability on the Korean Peninsula." These are the policies which were entirely eliminated under the former South Korean government of President Park Geun-hye, under intense pressure from President Obama.

President Moon Jae-in also addressed cooperation in the development of the Russian Far East, noting that his government had created a Northern Economic Cooperation Committee under his own leadership, to help make Korea a "leader in the development of the Far East. The Committee is tasked with strengthening economic cooperation with Northeast Asian and Eurasian countries." He added: "Next year, we will create a Korean-Russian Regional Cooperation Forum. It should

kremlin.ru

Vladimir Putin addressing the Eastern Economic Forum.

bolster contacts between regional governments in Korea and the Russian Far East."

Speaking at the Plenary Session, Moon said: "I propose to build nine bridges between Korea and Russia for simultaneous and multilateral cooperation." Among the nine bridges were gas, rail, the Northern Sea Route, shipbuilding and agriculture. Moon noted, "The world's first icebreaking liquefied natural-gas tanker was built by a Korean shipbuilding company and transferred to Russia, opening the era of the Northern Sea Route, which until then seemed to lie in the distant future."

Like Putin, Moon said the two had "agreed to build up the basis for the implementation of trilateral projects with participation of the two Korean states and Russia, which will connect the Korean Peninsula and the Russian Far East.... The development of the Far East will promote the prosperity of our two countries, and will also help change North Korea and create the basis for the implementation of the trilateral agreements. We will be working hard on this."

Following Putin's speech at the EEF, the North Korean delegate to the EEF, Minister of Foreign Economic Affairs Kim Yong Jae, said: "We are not opposed to trilateral cooperation, but this is not an appropriate situation for this to be implemented," referring to the threats coming from the U.S.

As to the war danger, both Putin and Moon were totally clear. In an interview with TASS, Moon said, "Our stance is firm—there should be no more wars on the Korean Peninsula. Nobody but Korea is in the posi-

President of the Republic of Korea Moon Jae-in (left) and Vladimir Putin making press statements following talks at the Eastern Economic Forum.

tion to decide if there may be war on the Korean Peninsula again. We have no intention of toppling the North Korean regime or achieving unification by means of a takeover. We seek to resolve the North Korean nuclear problem and to guarantee security to the North Korean regime. We wish to build a system of lasting peace in the Korean Peninsula. Also, we wish to create an economic community in which the South and the North might prosper together. This would be useful for the development of Russia's Far East, too."

For his part, Putin, speaking in his press conference at the end of the BRICS Summit, said: "Everyone remembers well what happened to Iraq and Saddam Hussein. Hussein abandoned the production of weapons of mass destruction. Nonetheless, under the pretext of searching for these weapons, Saddam Hussein himself and his family were killed during the well-known military operation. Even children died back then. His grandson, I believe, was shot to death. The country was destroyed, and Saddam Hussein was hanged. Listen, everyone is aware of it and everyone remembers it. North Koreans are also aware of it and remember it. Do you think that following the adoption of some sanctions, North Korea will abandon its course on creating weapons of mass destruction? Russia condemns these exercises on the part of North Korea. We believe they are provocative in nature. However, we cannot forget about what I just said about Iraq, and what happened later in Libya. Certainly, the North Koreans will not forget it. Sanctions of any kind are useless and ineffective in this case. As I said to one of my colleagues yesterday, 'they will eat grass, but they will not abandon this program unless they feel safe.'

"What can ensure security? The restoration of international law. We need to advance towards dialogue between all parties concerned. It is important for all participants in this process, including North Korea, not to have any thoughts about the threat of being destroyed; on the contrary, all sides to the conflict should cooperate. In this environment, in this situation, whipping up military hysteria is absolutely pointless; it is a dead end."

Interestingly, in the EEF Plenary Session, Putin said that he saw willingness on the part of the Trump Administration to ease tensions with North Korea. "We can see the current Administration's willingness to ease the situation," he said.

It is of note that the U.S. was represented at the EEF by 400 participants, including executives of ExxonMobil, IBM, and Abbott Laboratories. It should be obvious to American business interests that it is insane for the U.S. to be largely boycotting the biggest economic development process in history, on a global scale, because of the Obama Administration's demonization of Russia and his military and economic encirclement of China, through the Pivot to Asia and the Trans-Pacific Partnership (TPP).

Trump has pulled out of the TPP, and has made it clear that America's interests are best served by cooperation with Russia and China. A total of 217 agreements worth nearly $44 billion were signed at the EEF, according to the Russian presidential envoy to the Far East Federal District, Yury Trutnev. Unfortunately, none were with American firms.

Asia Moves Ahead

Other Great Projects are getting underway in Asia. On Monday, September 11, a major conference is being held in Bangkok on the building of the Kra Canal (now called the Thai Canal), involving several of the people who participated in a Kra Canal conference held in Bangkok in 1984, where Lyndon LaRouche was a keynote speaker along with leading political and scientific figures from Thailand, Japan, and across Asia. The project was delayed by a combination of political crises and the so-called Asian Financial Crisis of 1998. It has now gained new impetus from the Belt and Road Initiative, as it would be a key hub for the 21st Century Maritime Silk Road.

Africa: Transaqua Project Gains Momentum

by Claudio Celani

Sept. 9—After the historic memorandum of understanding between the Lake Chad Basin Commission (LCBC) and the Chinese giant PowerChina (see *EIR*, Jan. 6, 2017), further encouraging developments have fed the hope that finally, the 35-year-old Transaqua project for water-transfer, transport, energy and agro-industrial development in the Lake Chad region and Central Africa, will finally come to realization. On June 8, the Italian engineering firm Bonifica, which developed the Transaqua idea originally, signed a letter of intent with PowerChina in Hangzhou, for the joint exploration of the feasibility of the project.

Whereas the memorandum of understanding between the LCBC and PowerChina established "the basis on which the parties will carry out successful further research on the Lake Chad Basin Water Transfer Project and other future projects," the letter of intent between PowerChina and Bonifica includes the agree-

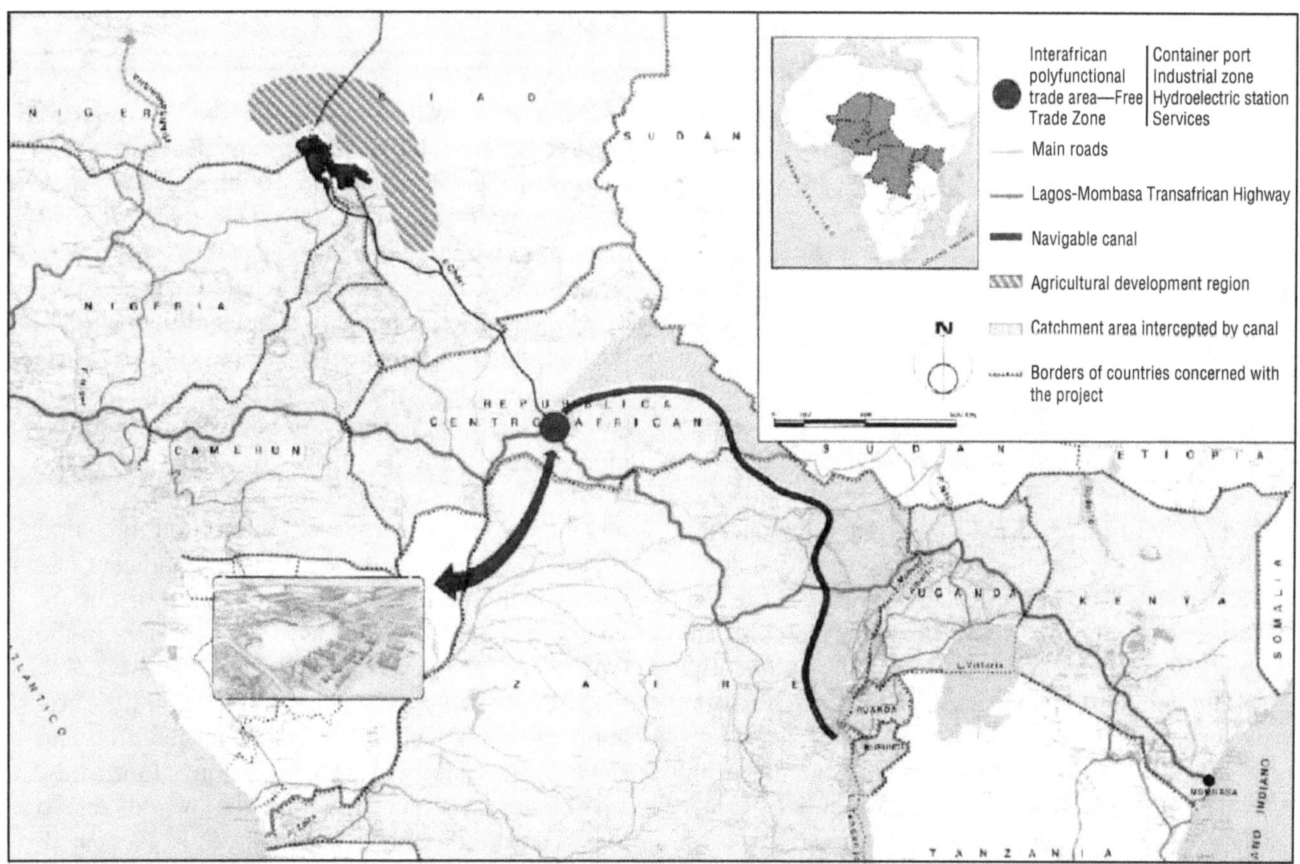

The blue ribbon is the canal that captures some of the water from the upper reaches of the Congo River tributaries in the yellow catchment area. The Congo River system itself is a background feature in pale blue, identified at its mouth as F. Zaire. The canal then feeds the water across the divide between the Congo and Chari basins and into the Chari River at the red spot; the Chari empties into Lake Chad.

Executive Secretary of the Lake Chad Basin Commission, Engineer Imran Sanusi Abdullahi (left) and Deputy Chief Engineer Zhy Ziping Huang of PowerChina in Djamena, Chad in March 2017.

ment "to cooperate in order to submit specific project proposals" based "on the thorough technical review and exchange of information concerning the Transaqua project."

The news of this agreement was first released by *EIR Strategic Alert Service* on Aug. 8, followed two days later by coverage in the Italian business daily *Il Sole 24 Ore*, which independently confirmed Italian Foreign Ministry interest in the project. Eventually, the Operations Portal of the UNHCR, the UN Agency for Refugees, posted the *EIR* story as picked up from the French *Solidarité et Progrès* website. Last but not least, the agreement was aptly covered by *People's Daily*, the official daily of the ruling Chinese Communist Party, which ran a lengthy article on Aug. 21, underscoring the key role played by Lyndon and Helga LaRouche in bringing the plan forward.

People's Daily quoted extensively from *EIR*, adding in its own words that "hopes have been revived for the 40 million people who depend on Lake Chad for their livelihoods," and: "Thanks to the fight taken up by LaRouche organization over the years and the initiators of Transaqua, the project is today be-

---

The Idea of Transaqua

The Transaqua idea is as simple as it is ingenious. Prompted by then-Bonifica CEO Francesco Curato, in 1972, a Bonifica team led by Dr. Marcello Vichi began to explore the idea of collecting enough water from the right-side tributaries of the Congo River, to refill Lake Chad and eventually develop hydroelectric power and irrigation potential. It was calculated that, to refill Lake Chad to its original dimensions, about 50 billion cubic meters of water would be needed. The Bonifica engineers envisioned the construction of a 2,400 km system of reservoirs and canals that would be able to collect 100 billion. This would amount to about 5-8% of the Congo River's water.

The Transaqua canal would start from the southeastern region of the Democratic Republic of Congo (DRC), intersect all the tributaries upstream, cross the DRC and the Central African Republic (CAR), and reach the watershed between the CAR and Chad at about 500 meters altitude. Here, it would pour into the Chari River, which feeds Lake Chad, having carried 100 billion cubic meters of water per year, purely by gravity, in a 10-meter deep, 100-meter wide canal. It would really be a new, manmade river, with dimensions comparable to the Nile at the Aswan dam.

Along its path, Transaqua would create systems of reservoirs, water regulation and hydropower production that would benefit every basin of the Congo's tributaries, without negatively affecting their carrying capacity, fisheries, or navigability. Furthermore, a road would be built as necessary to serve the construction of the canal-dams system, which would remain as a modern transport connection in central Africa. The canal itself would be a magnificent waterway, with the idea of building at least one major inland port and economic development area in the CAR.

The new irrigation potential would allow the creation of an agricultural development area around Lake Chad as large as the Italian region of Lombardy.

The construction of Transaqua would absorb hundreds of thousands of unemployed workers in all the central African nations, providing them with an income and creating a demand for goods and materials from throughout the continent.

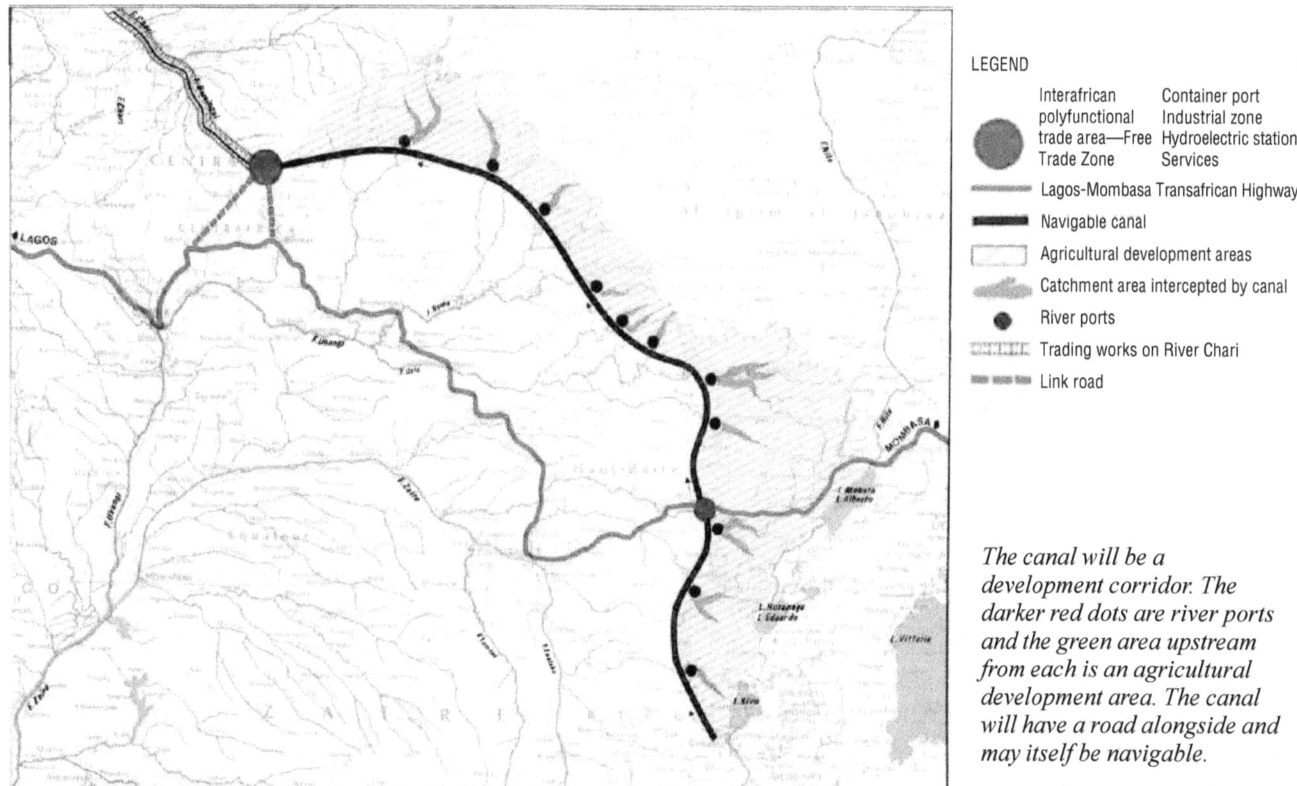

The canal will be a development corridor. The darker red dots are river ports and the green area upstream from each is an agricultural development area. The canal will have a road alongside and may itself be navigable.

coming reality within the framework of the Belt and Road Initiative. *Executive Intelligence Review* magazine and Schiller Institute in 2015 arranged the first meeting between LCBC and the brains behind Transaqua. This was followed in December 2016 by the signing of the Memorandum of Understanding between LCBC and PowerChina, and subsequent contacts between Bonifica Spa and the Chinese company." The *People's Daily* article was republished by former U.S. diplomat David H. Shinn on his widely read blog: http://davidshinn.blogspot.de/2017/08/chinese-a nd-italian-companies-agree-on.html

The idea of Transaqua has been around for over 35 years, but things have started to move only recently, thanks to two factors: China's fight for the development of Africa (as an extension of its Belt and Road policy) and the refugee crisis. The latter has made it very clear that only by creating jobs and development in Africa, can the refugee wave to Europe be stopped.

Italy, at the forefront of the refugee flow and abandoned by its European "allies" to face the crisis alone, has now developed an interest in Transaqua. According to *EIR* sources, Italian Prime Minister Paolo Gentiloni raised the issue at the summit with his colleagues from France, Germany, and Spain on Aug. 28, telling them that the Italian Foreign Ministry is examining a plan for Lake Chad.

According to *EIR*'s information, the Italian Foreign Ministry is even considering financing the 3 million euro feasibility study with COP24 ("climate change") funds. However, the required bureaucratic procedures may take too long, so that it might be faster to find other funding sources outside of Italy.

Transaqua Enemies Attack LaRouches

The momentum in favor of Transaqua has raised hopes for Africa, but fear for imperial interests. A putatively Congolese network which had already attacked Transaqua in 2014, has now attacked it again with a long article full of falsities and slanders. The authors of Transaqua and its sponsors are accused of aiming to "steal Congo's water," and create an ecological catastrophe by transferring 5% of the Congo River's water to Lake Chad. They claim Transaqua is a new form of European looting of African resources. They attacked Lyndon and Helga LaRouche and Jacques Cheminade, the leader of LaRouche's co-thinker organization in France.

But it is the authors of the attack who should explain their own ties to the interests that have historically looted and still loot Africa.

Author Sinaseli Tshibwabwa, in fact, is a biologist who is based in Kinshasa, but his neomalthusian ideology is made in Europe. In fact, at the beginning of his article he quotes Géraud Magrin, a professor at the Sorbonne, who even claims that the shrinking of Lake Chad is an invention by those who want to build environmentally hostile water-transfer projects.

The article is published in an outlet run by a certain Jean-Jacques Wondo, another Congolese national, who graduated from the Royal Military Academy in Belgium, got his master's at Liege University, and did graduate work at the Free University of Brussels. https://desc-wondo.org/en/after-plundering-minerals-soon-the-plundering-of-the-congo-freshwater-the-blue-gold-of-this-century-sinaseli-tshi bwabwa/

It is worth refuting one argument here: that Transaqua, by taking 5% of the water from the Congo River's tributaries, would reduce the amount of electric power generated by the proposed Grand Inga project in the Democratic Republic of the Congo (DRC). This argument is also circulating among African diplomats, but the problem does not exist: In fact, that 5% of the water would also produce electricity, but on the eastern side of the DRC, thus saving the costs of transmission from Inga, which is situated in the westernmost part, close to the Congo estuary.

The other arguments and the falsehoods about Transaqua were already answered by Transaqua author Marcello Vichi in 2014, with a long letter to the editor of the 7sur7 website. This time, Bonifica CEO Mrs. Romina Boldrini issued a statement to *EIR* Aug. 29, in which, among other things, she makes it very clear that "currently, Transaqua is not a developed and approved project, which, regardless of the will of countries and peoples, has been imposed on African countries: *it is an opportunity*. The opportunity of assessing and developing a solution that could allow all concerned parties to consciously criticize, modify, accept, and share the proposed solution—or to propose another one."

Jacques Cheminade answered with a long letter to MoviSol.org in which, among other things, he exposed those who oppose water-transfer projects that would save millions of African lives, and reminded them that he "supported in France the elimination of the CFA franc [a French-controlled African currency], to allow African countries to regain their monetary sovereignty and allow them to issue credit for their infrastructure, their industry and their agricultural development."

Transaqua: Bonifica Answers the Critics

In a statement released to *EIR* Aug. 29, Bonifica CEO Romina Boldrini answered recent criticisms and slanders against the Transaqua project for water-transfer from the Congo Basin to the Lake Chad Basin, and associated infrastructural development.

"Concerning recent media reports on the Transaqua project," her statement says, "I felt it opportune, as a legal representative of Bonifica Spa, to at least present our views on the matter. To express one's own opinion and point of view is a human right, even when it is contrary to someone else's ideas and positions.

"However, I believe it is necessary to avoid producing sterile polemics, for their own sake, without a solution: I think that an objective analysis of facts is more difficult but more constructive and conclusive, and the best offer to the reader and to those who are directly involved in the process."

"In this regard, Bonifica has some merit: having exposed, for over thirty years now, the dimension of the emergency, explored a myriad of possible solutions, and identified one possible organic solution after having warned at an early stage about demographic growth in Nigeria, and about the social-economic crisis of a very large area. Bonifica did this alone."

"Let us now forget for a moment that we have been the 'fathers of the Transaqua project' and try to offer the most objective possible point of view.

"The facts:

• It is indisputable that Lake Chad is undergoing an irreversible process of desertification. It suffices to see the satellite data related to the Lake Chad basin. Such a process is generated by a series of interconnected causes, and can be interrupted only through an extraordinary and permanent intervention;

• It is indisputable that this situation is leading to climatic changes that affect both vegetation and wildlife in the area;

• It is indisputable that the population—and not only the population—is threatened by starvation because of the progressive shrinking of Lake Chad: The lack of opportunities for support and jobs, and the increasing poverty, have tragic consequences, both in terms of public health and socially, with the development of terrorist phenomena;

• It is indisputable that the population in that area has a continuous demographic growth; this not only aggravates the situation, but increases ever more the flow of migration towards other areas.

"But confronting these facts, there are opportunities:

• The opportunity of relying, today more than before, on international aid. Immigration and terrorism are violently striking the so-called 'Western World,' which finally, and perhaps for its own egoistic reasons, is looking at Africa's problems today, as its own problems;

• The opportunity to examine and develop some project-ideas, among them Transaqua, for the purpose of considering the best solution or solutions to adopt in order to help to solve one among the many problems in Africa. Here we must open a necessary chapter:

Transaqua is not a project that was developed independently of the will of the countries involved.

Transaqua is not a project which was imposed on the African countries involved.

Transaqua is a project idea, studied and developed in its pre-feasibility stage already in the 1980s, and, at that time, approved and shared by the then President of Congo (former Zaire).

Transaqua is an ambitious project because the emergency in Africa has a planetary dimension, such that it cannot be faced with modest projects or, worse, with short-term solutions.

Transaqua is a possible solution 'on the table,' which should be developed through a feasibility study in order to understand and assess a series of aspects:

Technical feasibility
Economic-financial feasibility
Environmental impact
Agreement of the states concerned
Its economic and social benefits
Critical aspects.

"Currently, Transaqua is not a developed and approved project which, regardless of the will of countries and peoples, has been imposed on African countries: *it is an opportunity*. The opportunity of assessing and developing a solution that could allow all concerned parties to consciously criticize, modify, accept and share the proposed solution—or to propose another one.

"The opportunity, this is the keystone. Without opportunities there are no chances, there are no solutions.

"This is what we want to offer to African countries: the opportunity to have in their hands the feasibility study of a project, financed by western countries and/or international agencies, which could allow us to offer a potential solution."

LARGEST MEXICAN EARTHQUAKE IN A CENTURY

Time to Forecast Natural Disasters And Defend Mankind!

by Benjamin L. Deniston

EDITORIAL

Sept. 10—Late August into early September has been a tumultuous time in our Solar system. The United States, Mexico, and the Caribbean are being slammed by a series of intense hurricanes (Harvey, Irma, José, and Katia). Prior to the hurricanes, the Sun released several explosive solar flares (including the largest in over a decade) and launched bursts of plasma directly at the Earth, extents that generated severe geomagnetic storms. In addition to the hurricanes, Mexico was rocked by the largest earthquake in over a century—a magnitude 8.1 quake 90 km off the southwest coast.

These natural events remind us of mankind's vulnerability to the hazards in our Solar system, and underscore the strategic reality of our times: Nations must come together to defend Earth from these threats.

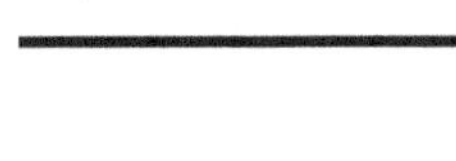

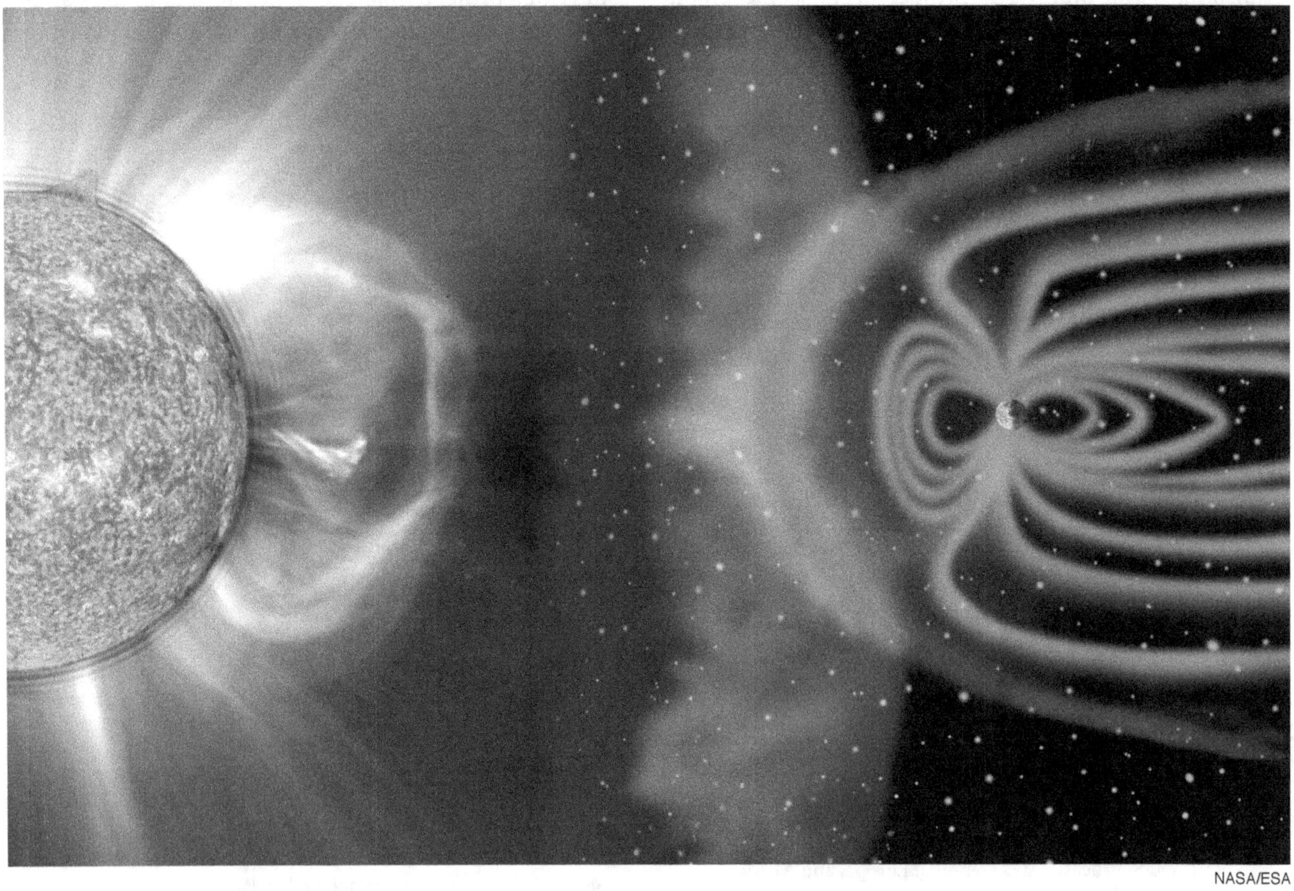

NASA/ESA

Solar events can be monitored for their potential to cause severe geomagnetic events. Here, a coronal mass ejection is about to lift off from the Sun. In this artist's rendition, Earth and the field lines of its magnetosphere are at right.

The magnitude 8.1 Chiapas earthquake has tragically taken about 100 lives (according to information available on Sept. 10). Thanks to electrical sensors and warning systems, many residents were given a warning a few tens of seconds before the earthquake waves reached them—providing just enough time to exit buildings, or find shelter. But what if we could provide warnings hours, or even days before major earthquakes strike?

For decades, small groups of pioneering scientists have dedicated themselves to detecting, studying, and understanding precursor signals that appear in the hours, days, and weeks before the eruption of seismic events. These scientists have shown that various forms of electrical, electromagnetic, magnetic, thermal, and other anomalies and signals precede earthquakes, providing the basis for early warning systems that could save countless lives.

One of the leading pioneers in this area is Professor Sergey Pulinets, who has presented his revolutionary work to *EIR*, the Schiller Institute, and LaRouche PAC. Professor Pulinets has collaborated with his colleague Professor Dimitar Ouzounov in the development of their lithosphere-atmosphere-ionosphere coupling model. This model explains the physics behind earthquake precursor signals, and provides the theoretical framework for an earthquake early-warning system.

After extensive study and demonstration, their team is ready to bring this work into active application—if governments are ready to step forward and support the development of earthquake early-warning systems.

Presently, the leadership of China, Russia, the Belt and Road Initiative, and the BRICS partnership is bringing the world closer to the New Paradigm envisioned by Helga and Lyndon LaRouche. Strategically, this means that these leading powers, including those in Europe and the U.S.A., must abandon geopolitical ambitions, and engage in strategic collaboration to defend the Earth and all its inhabitants from the challenges that threaten all mankind.

We must collaborate in forecasting earthquakes and volcanic eruptions; we must defend Earth from asteroids and comets; we must learn to control extreme weather events; we must collaborate in the defense of that one humanity which we all share.

www.ingramcontent.com/pod-product-compliance
Lightning Source LLC
Chambersburg PA
CBHW080734260726
48660CB00010B/3836